B is for Boner

A Hand Lettering

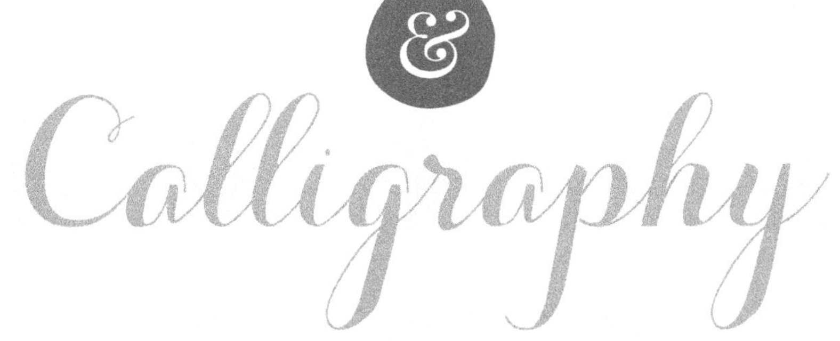

Workbook FOR

NAUGHTY ADULTS

This sexy calligraphy book belongs to:

____

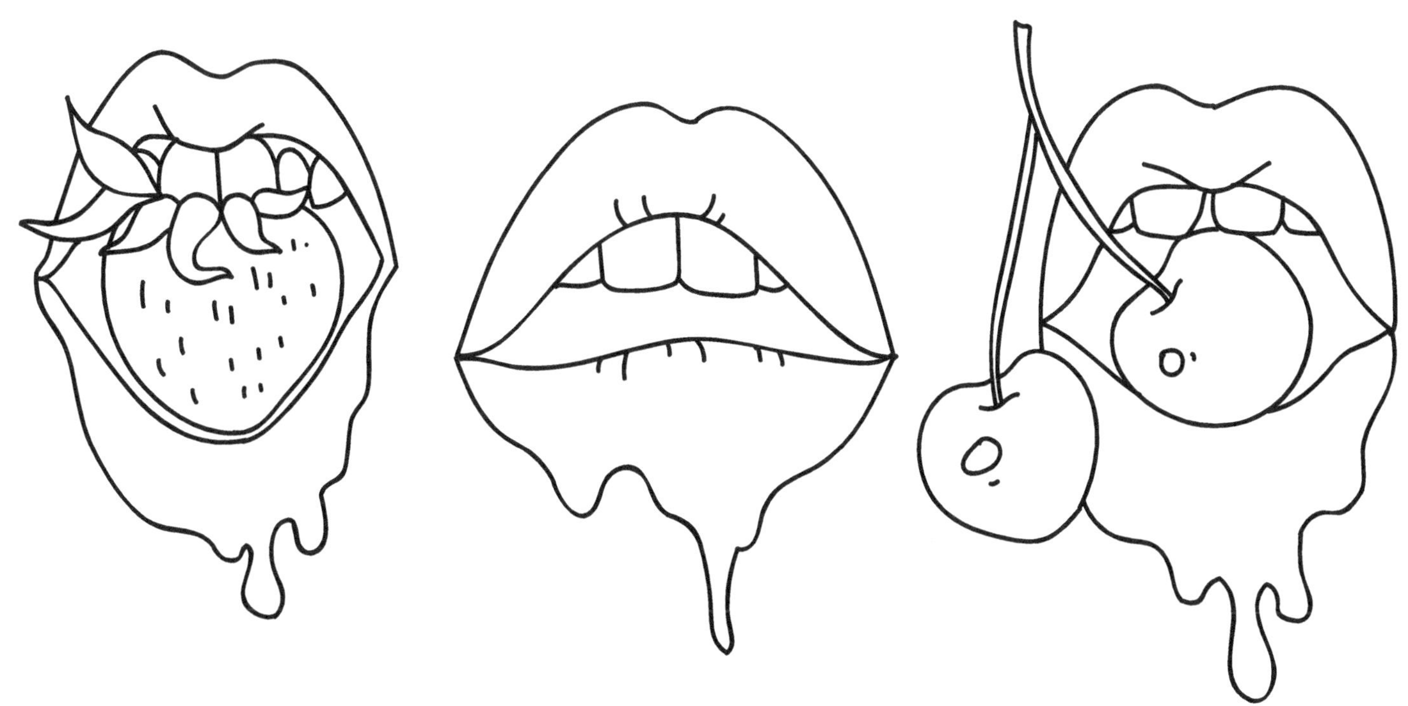

Intro

Thank you for buying this book! You are on your way to learning a new skill that could be the start of a new career, a new hobby, or just plain fun. This book is a simple and easy to use guide to help you practice the basic shapes and strokes involved in hand-lettering. This is an informational tool in a workbook style so you can start your practice today! Please be sure to read and practice every step as we all know that the only way to get better at anything is to practice, practice, practice!

History

The art of "Hand-lettering" has its roots in the ancient cave drawings of our ancestors and has been developed over thousands of years with the creation of letterforms to represent language. Classic calligraphy using a broad stroke pen was used in the Middle Ages up until Medieval times and fell out of favor around the 20th century. However, Calligraphy and Hand-lettering as an artform is making a huge comeback. Today, Modern Calligraphy is a combination of the classic brushstrokes from centuries ago, combined with the artist's own personal flair.

Uses

There are eight fonts we are going to practice in this book, all of which are the Modern Calligraphy style. Modern Calligraphy has become very popular for various reasons and is most easily known for its cursive style. Take your time with each font, practice letters, words, and numbers carefully. Once you perfect your craft, there are many opportunities for careers in Hand-Lettering. Modern Calligraphers or Hand-Lettering Artists have careers that range from Graphic Designers to Typographers, to Custom Sign Painters on buildings and for signs used in Advertising. So pick up your pen and see where it takes you!

Supplies

Hand-lettering can be done with a number of different pens and makers such as a traditional steel-head dip pen or a regular paintbrush. However, for our practice, we recommend using a brush pen for the Modern font. Brush pens are basically markers where the tip is shaped and feels like the head of a paintbrush. They come in many different sizes and range from soft to hard. The larger the marker the bigger the letters so I recommend a medium sized brush head with medium softness for beginners. For the chisel tip marker, try to find a "2.0" in size. As you continue your practice, feel free to play around with different options until you find the one that works for you!

Form

The secret to mastering any new skill is learning the proper form from the start. Make sure you are sitting in a comfortable position with your writing arm at a 90° angle and hold your wrist straight. **Brush Pen:** Using the brush pen for the Modern font, hold the pen as you would any other writing object, but rotate your entire arm including your wrist ever so slightly to the right if you write with your right and vice-versa for the left. The head of the pen should be at a slight angle when it hits the paper. When moving the pen down and then up across the paper, you want to move your entire arm with the pen, not just your wrist. You can do this by keeping your wrist straight and not bent in either direction. For a thick brushstroke, also referred to as a broadstroke, press down on the pen on the downstroke. For a thin or hairline stroke, lightly kiss the paper with the tip of the pen on the upstroke as you gently lift the pen off the paper. To remember this, you can think "Press - Down. Lift - Up." **Chisel tip Marker:** Using the chisel tip marker, follow the same form as above, however, rotate the head of the marker until it is 45 degrees when it hits the paper. Keep the pen at this angle at all times! You will notice that this will give you a thick stroke on the downstroke and a thinner stroke on the upstroke and side strokes. Pay attention to the direction of the strokes when writing each letter! If this doesn't come easy to you, remember to practice, practice, practice! Your work will improve with the proper form.

Basic Parts in Typography

EXAMPLE

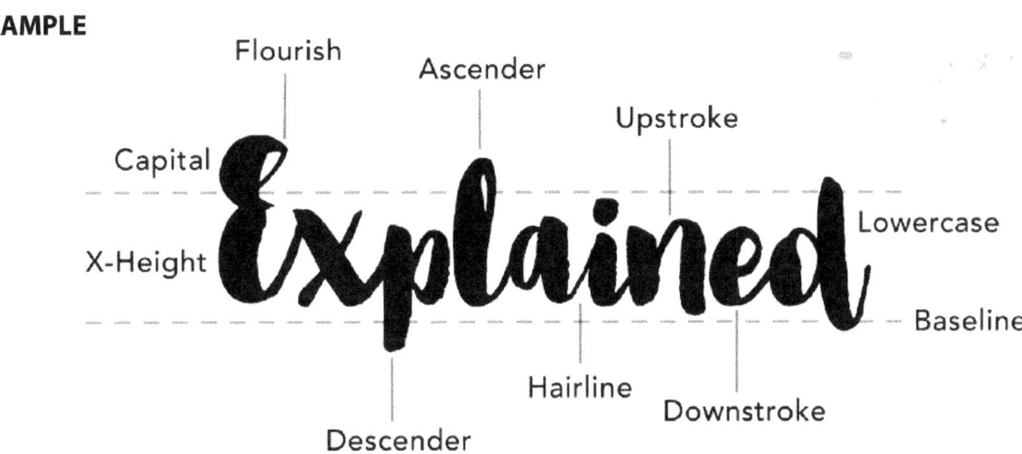

ASCENDER - The part of a lowercase letter that extends above the base
BASELINE - The imaginary line upon which a line of text rests
CAPITAL - A letter of the alphabet that differs in size, specifically height, from its corresponding lowercase letter, in that it is larger and taller.
DESCENDER - The part of a lowercase letter that extends below the base
DOWNSTROKE - A downward stroke made by a pen
FLOURISH - A waving movement, or an extra decoration on a letter
HAIRLINE - The thinnest line of a letter, commonly the upstroke in hand-lettering
LOWERCASE - A letter of the alphabet that differs in size, specifically height, from its corresponding uppercase letter, in that it is smaller and shorter.
UPSTROKE - An upward stroke made by a pen
X-HEIGHT - The height of lowercase letters in a font based on the height of the lowercase letter x

Start Practicing →

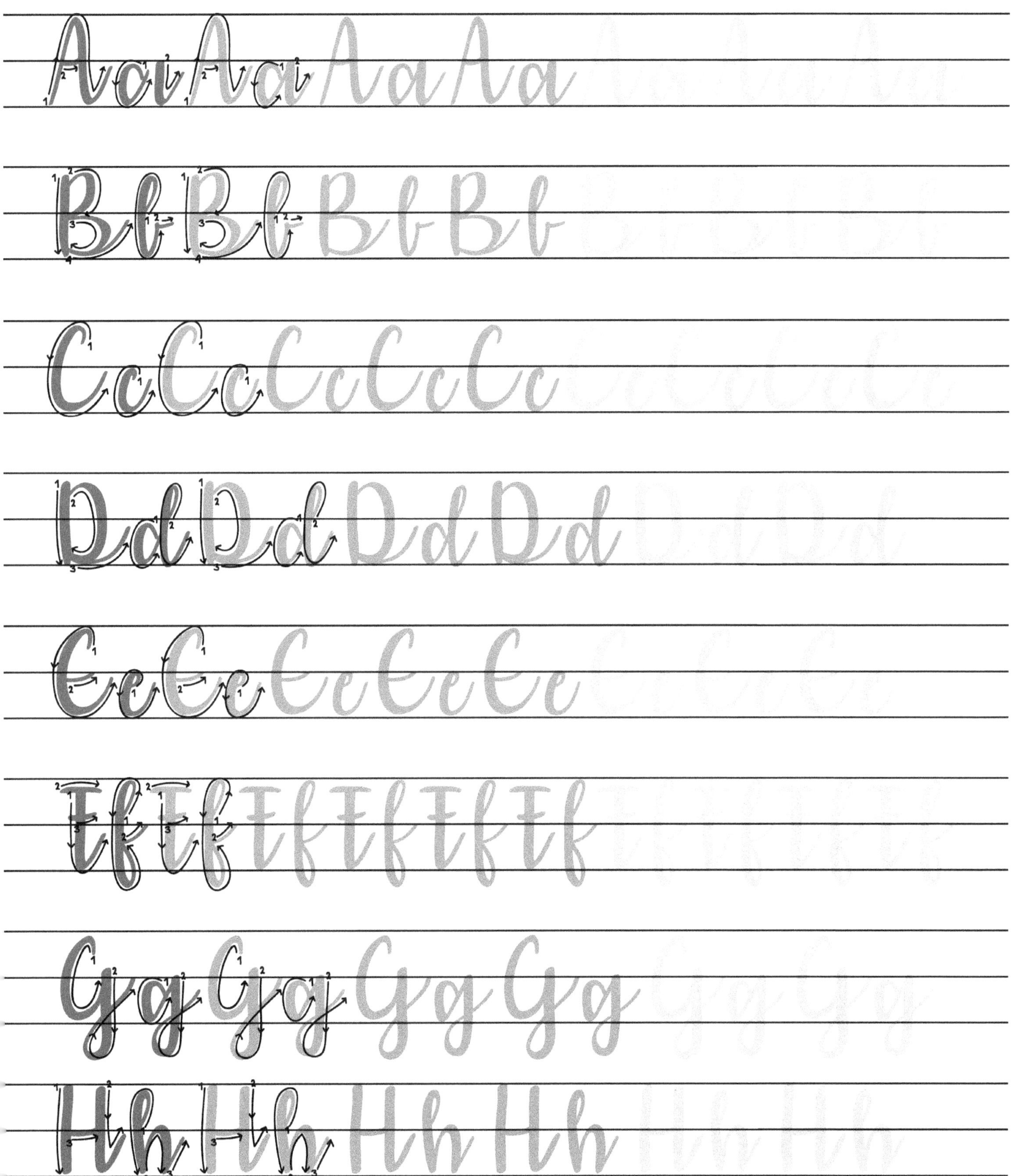

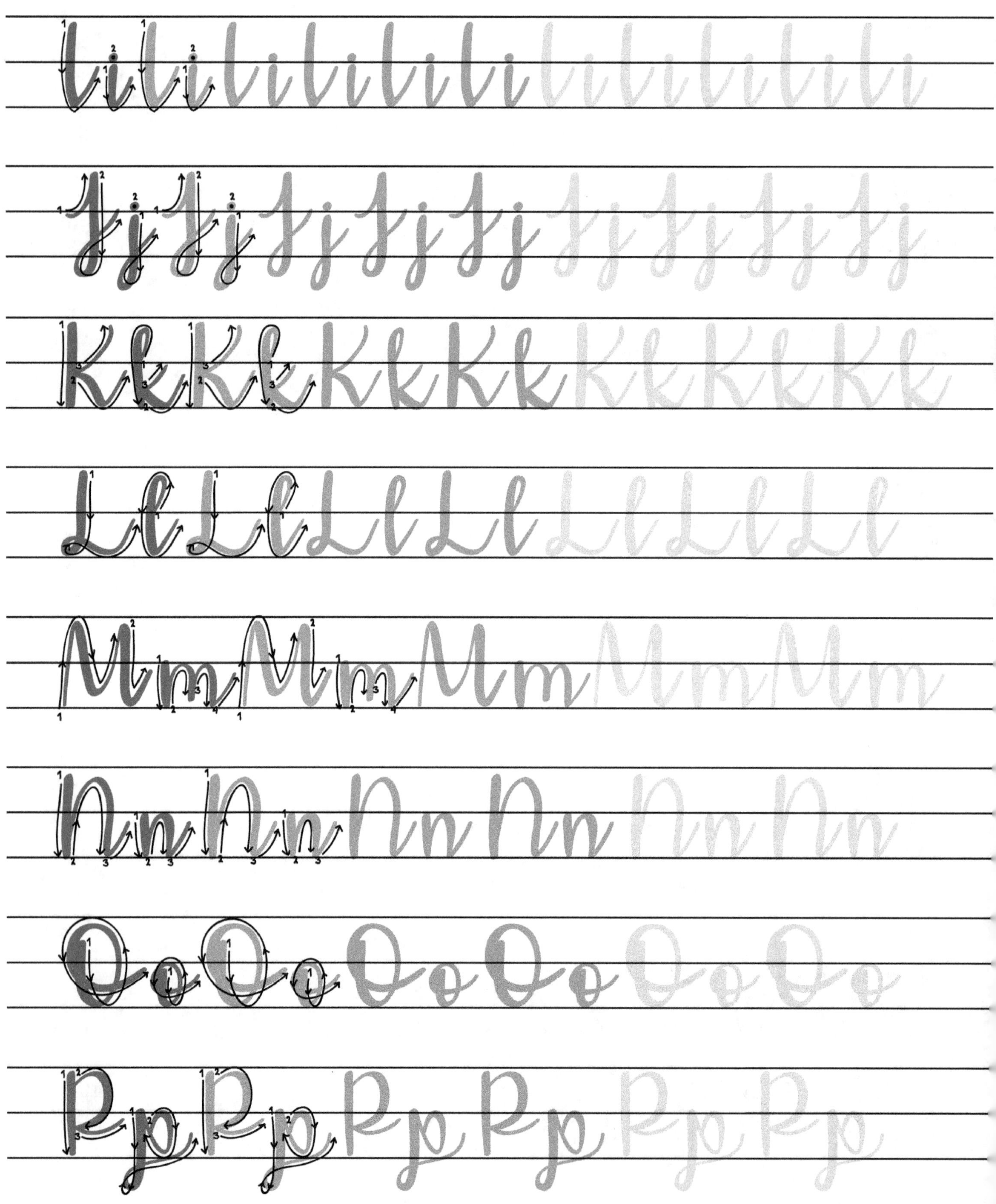

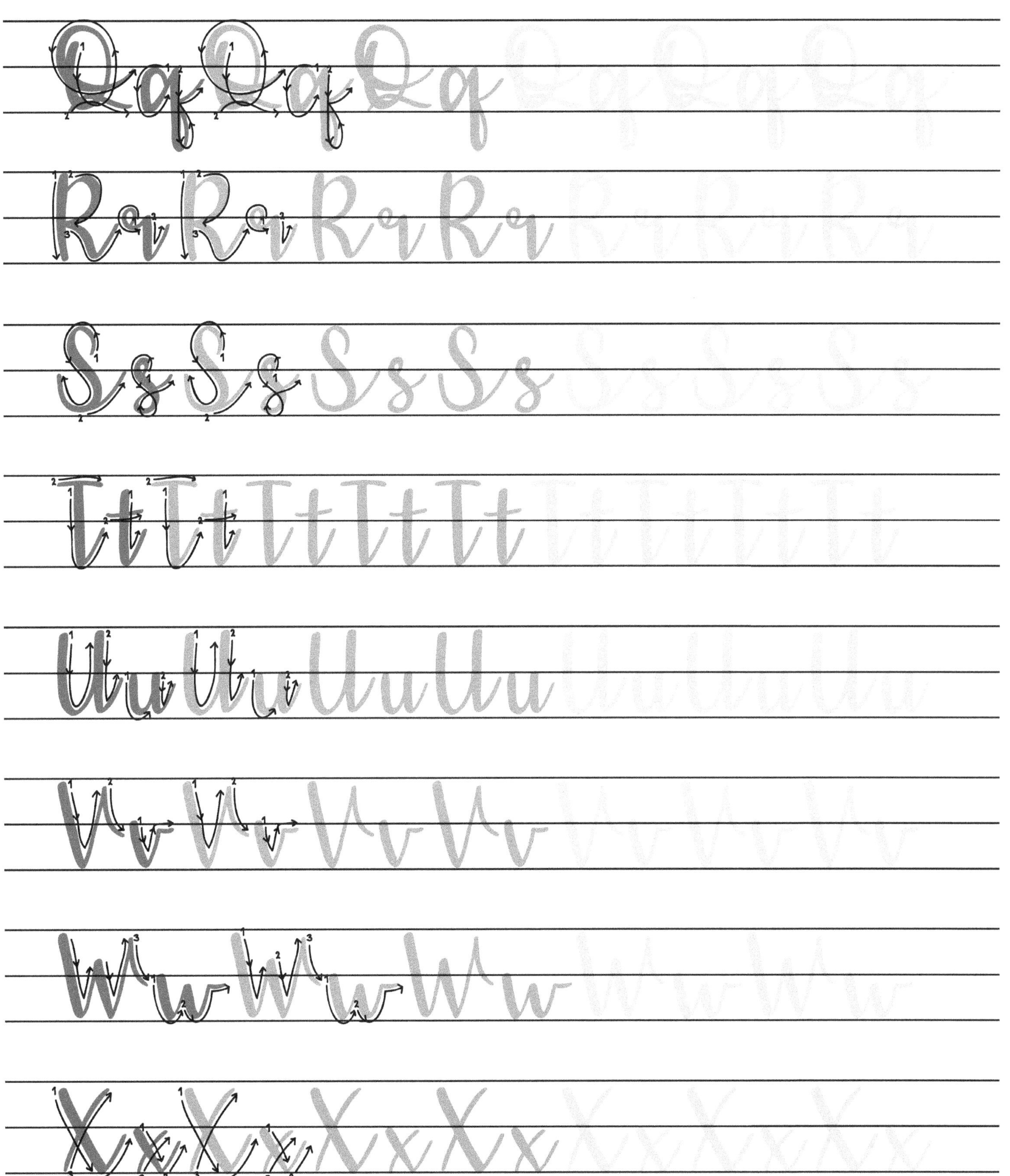

0000000 11111111

2222222 3333333

4444444 5555555

6666666 7777777

8888888 9999999

January January

January January

February February

February February

March March March

March March March

April April April April

April April April April

May May May May

May May May May

June June June June

June June June June

July July July July

July July July July

August August August

August August August

September September

September September

October October October

October October October

November November

November November

December December

December December

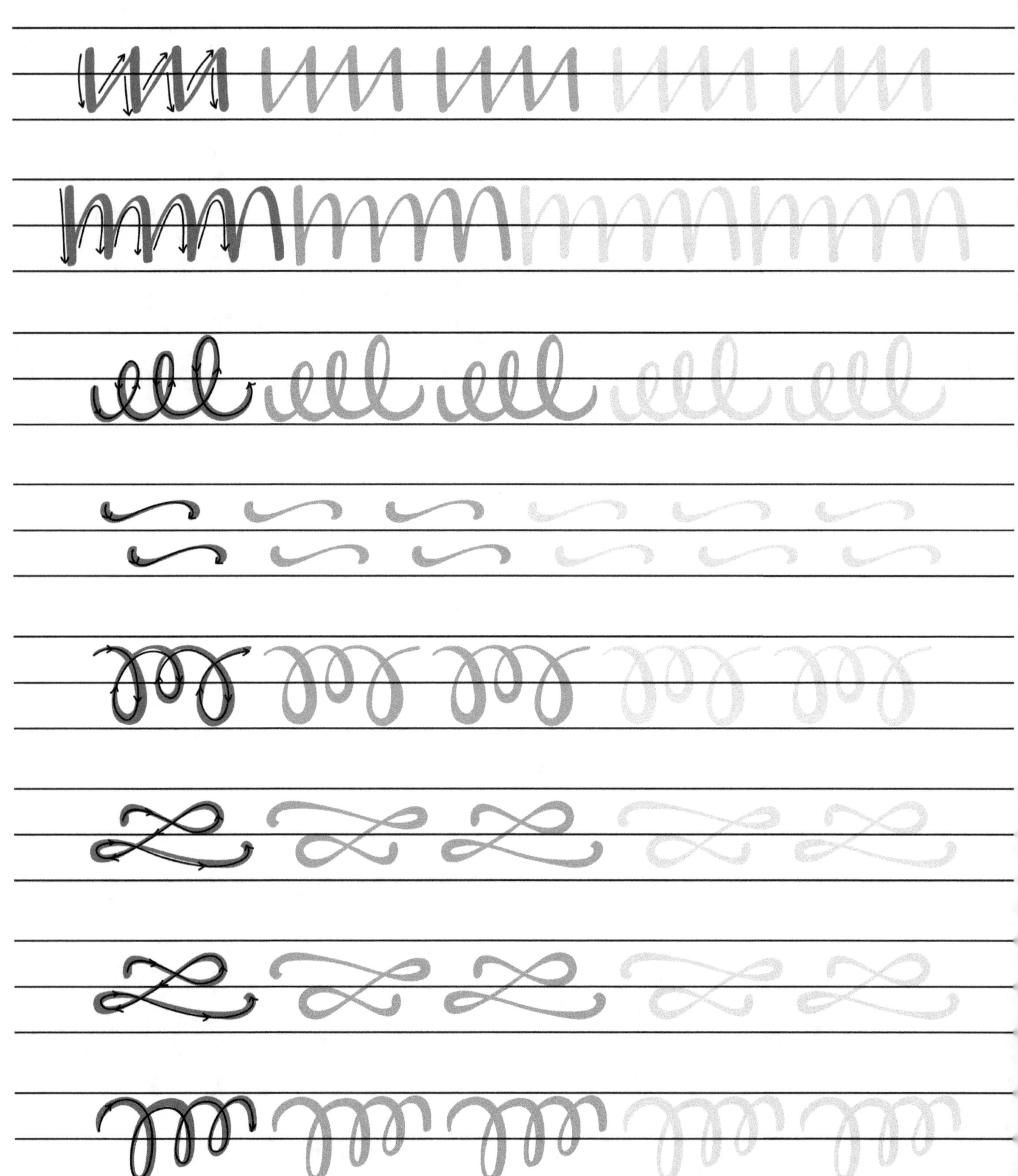

Ass Ass Ass Ass

Ass Ass Ass Ass

Anal Anal Anal

Anal Anal Anal

Boner Boner Boner

Boner Boner Boner

Booty call Booty call

Booty call Booty call

Bondage Bondage

Bondage Bondage

Blow job Blow job

Blow job Blow job

Clit Clit Clit Clit

Clit Clit Clit Clit

Cum Cum Cum

Cum Cum Cum

Cock ring Cock ring

Cock ring Cock ring

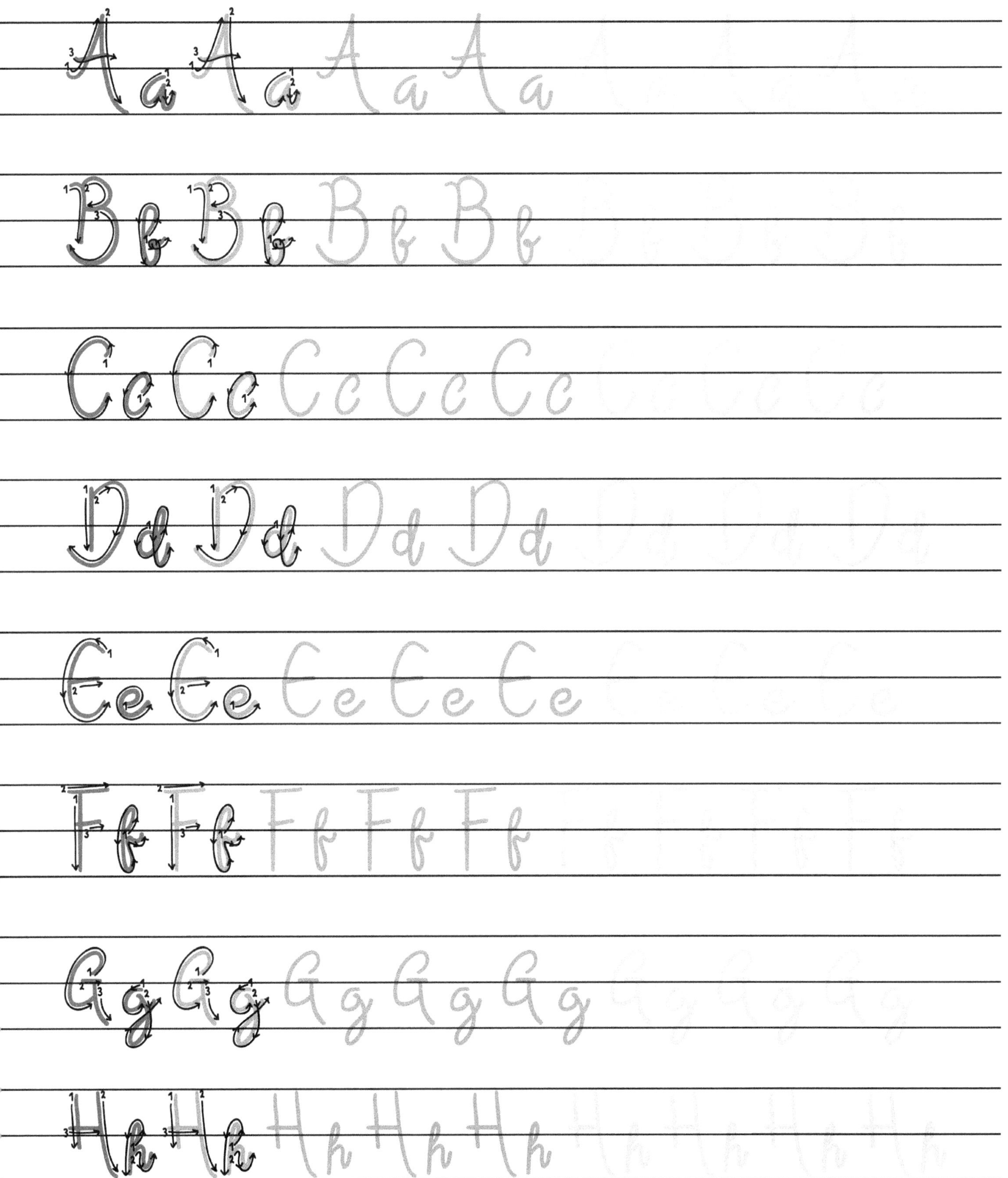

Ii Ii Ii Ii Ii Ii Ii Ii Ii

Jj Jj Jj Jj Jj Jj Jj Jj Jj

Kk Kk Kk Kk Kk Kk Kk Kk Kk

Ll Ll Ll Ll Ll Ll Ll Ll Ll

Mm Mm Mm Mm Mm Mm Mm Mm

Nn Nn Nn Nn Nn Nn Nn Nn Nn

Oo Oo Oo Oo Oo Oo Oo Oo Oo Oo

Pp Pp Pp Pp Pp Pp Pp Pp Pp Pp

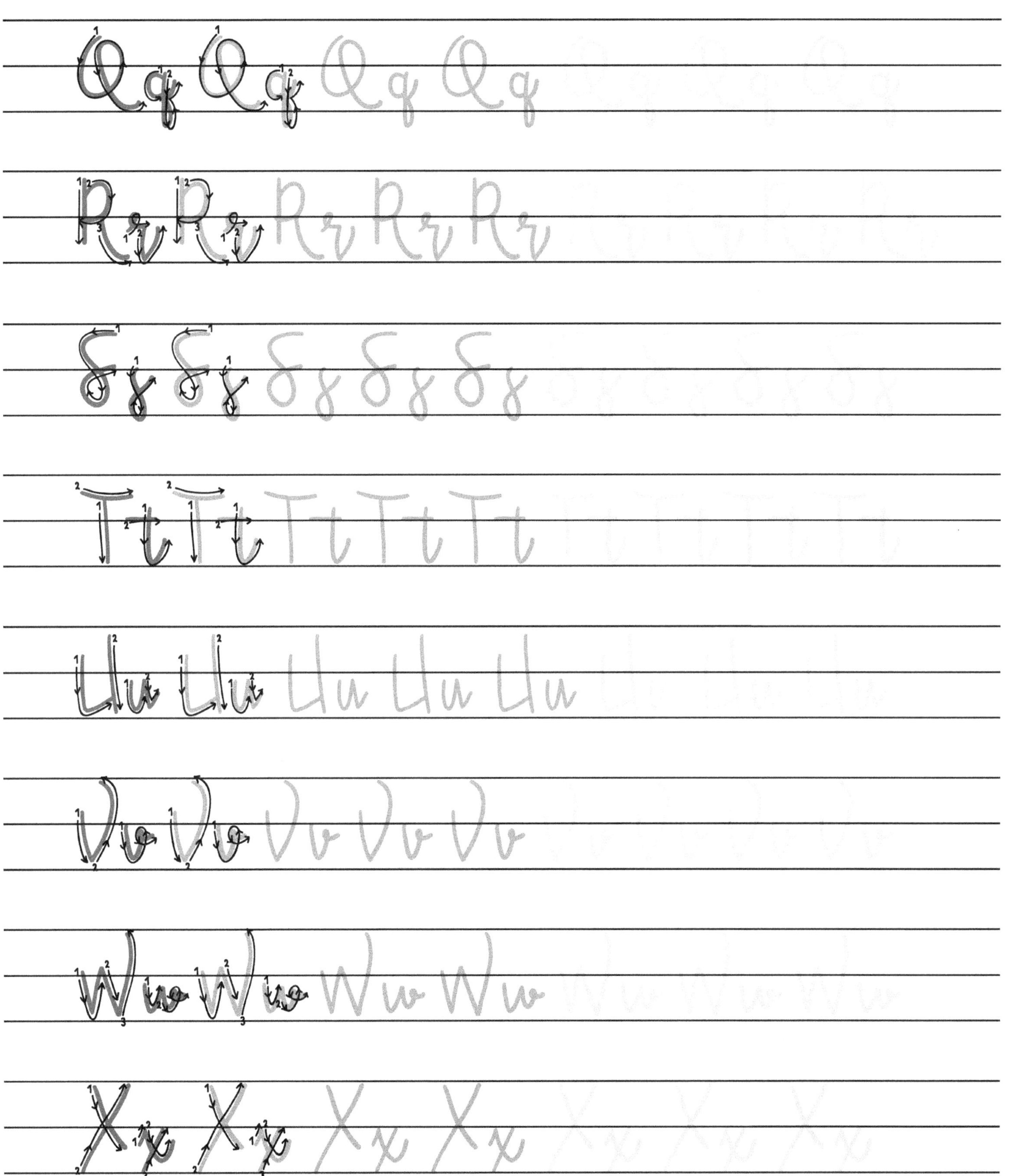

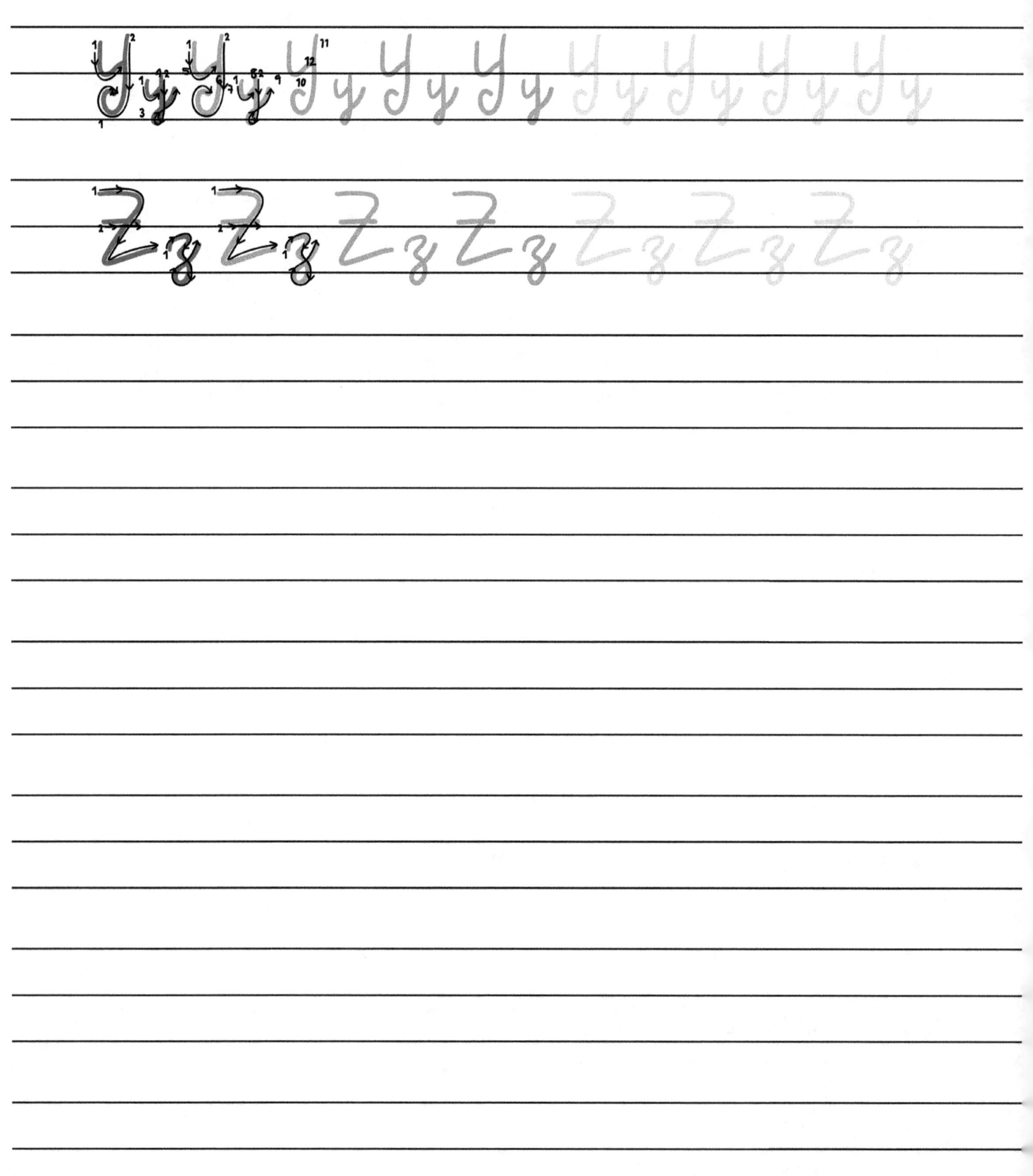

00000000 11111111

22222222 33333333

44444444 55555555

66666666 77777777

88888888 99999999

January January

January January

February February

February February

March March March

March March March

April April April

April April April

May May May May

May May May May

June June June June

June June June June

July July July July

July July July July

August August August

August August August

September September

September September

October October October

October October October

November November

November November

December December

December December

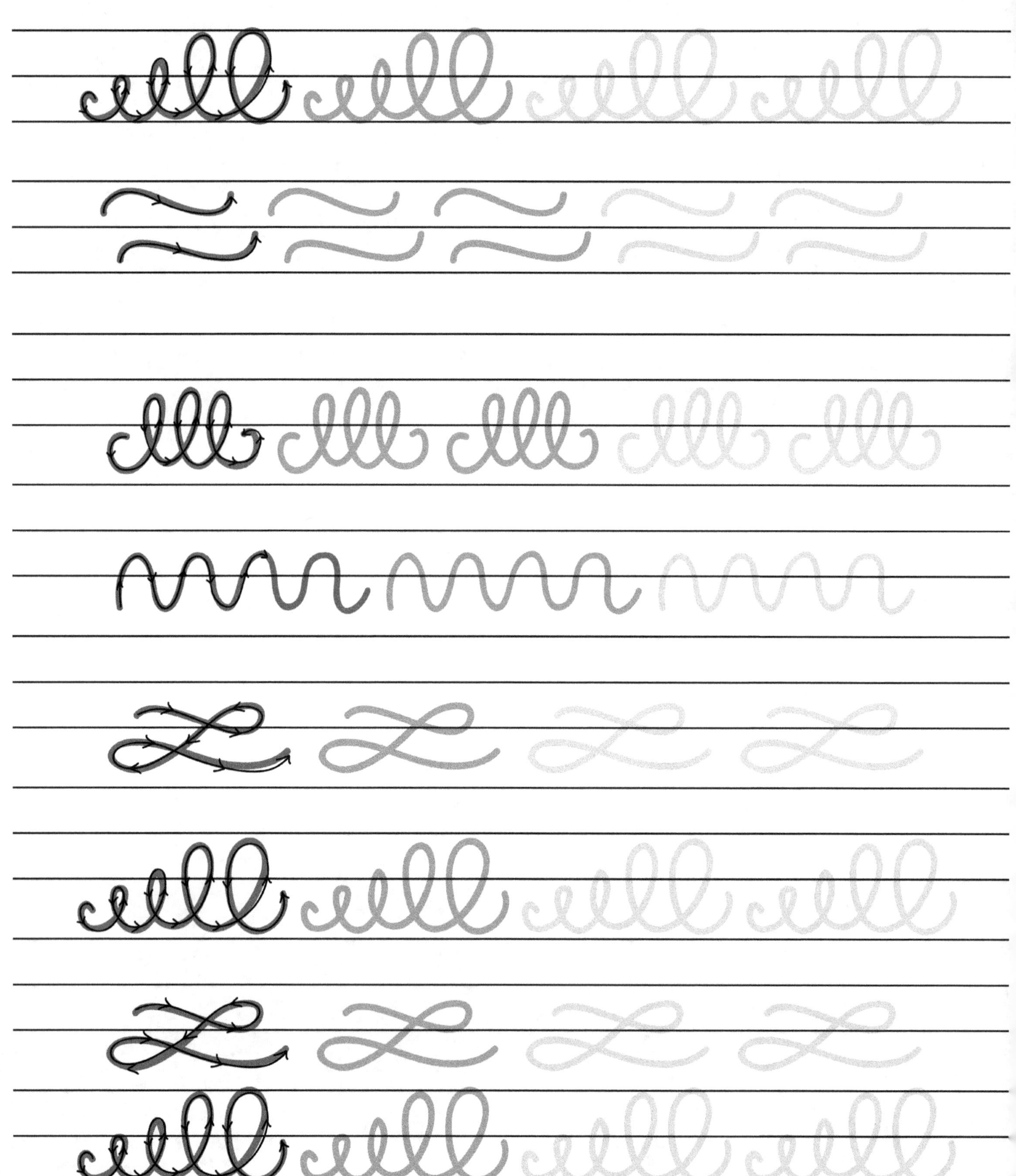

Dick Dick Dick

Dick Dick Dick

Dildo Dildo Dildo

Dildo Dildo Dildo

Erection Erection

Erection Erection

Fantasy Fantasy

Fantasy Fantasy

Fuck Fuck Fuck

Fuck Fuck Fuck

Foreplay Foreplay

Foreplay Foreplay

Fingering Fingering

Fingering Fingering

Girth Girth Girth

Girth Girth Girth

G-Spot G-Spot G-Spot

G-Spot G-Spot G-Spot

Ii Ii Ii Ii Ii

Jj Jj Jj Jj Jj

Kk Kk Kk Kk

Ll Ll Ll Ll Ll

Mm Mm Mm Mm

Nn Nn Nn Nn

Oo Oo Oo Oo

Pp Pp Pp Pp Pp

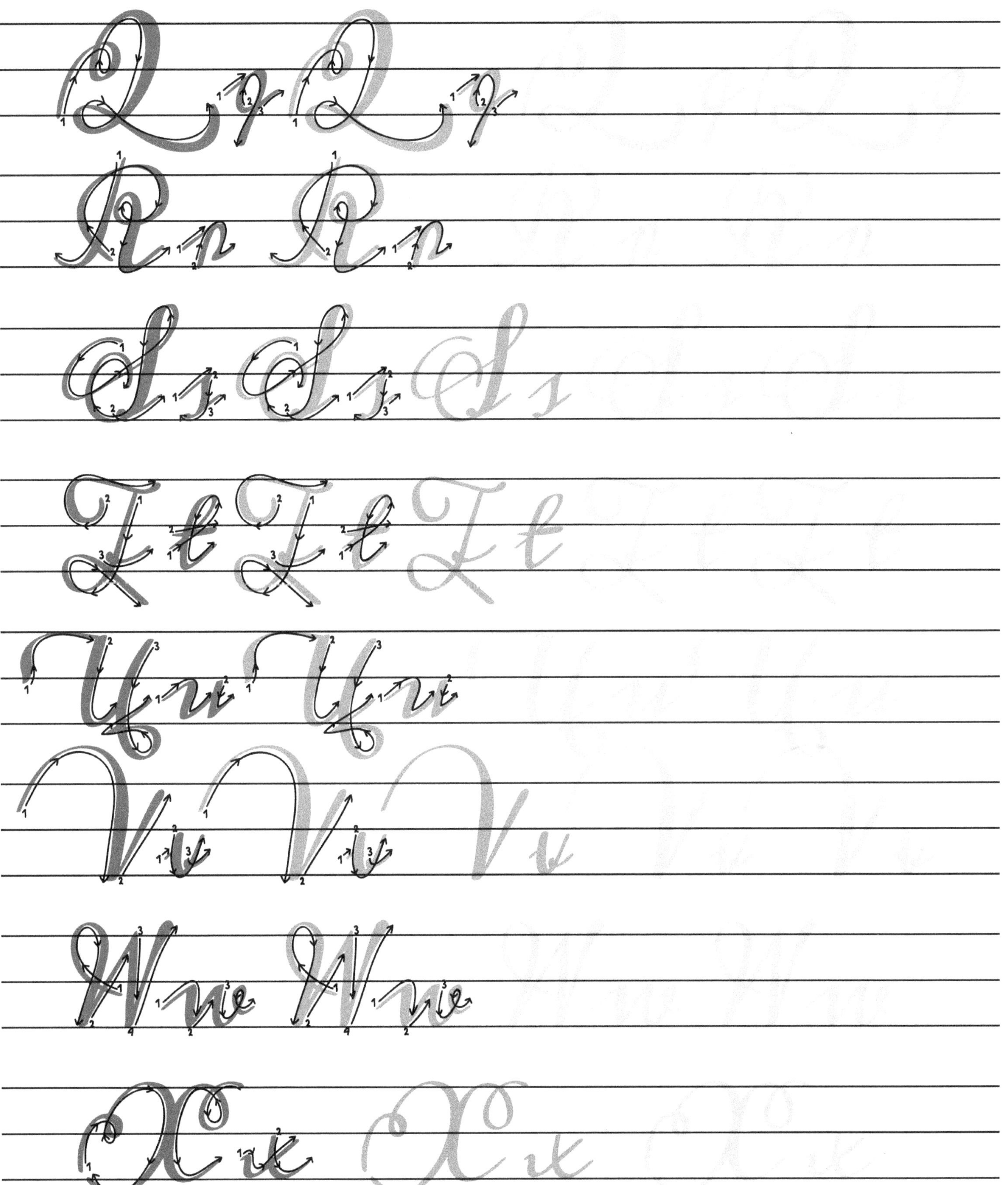

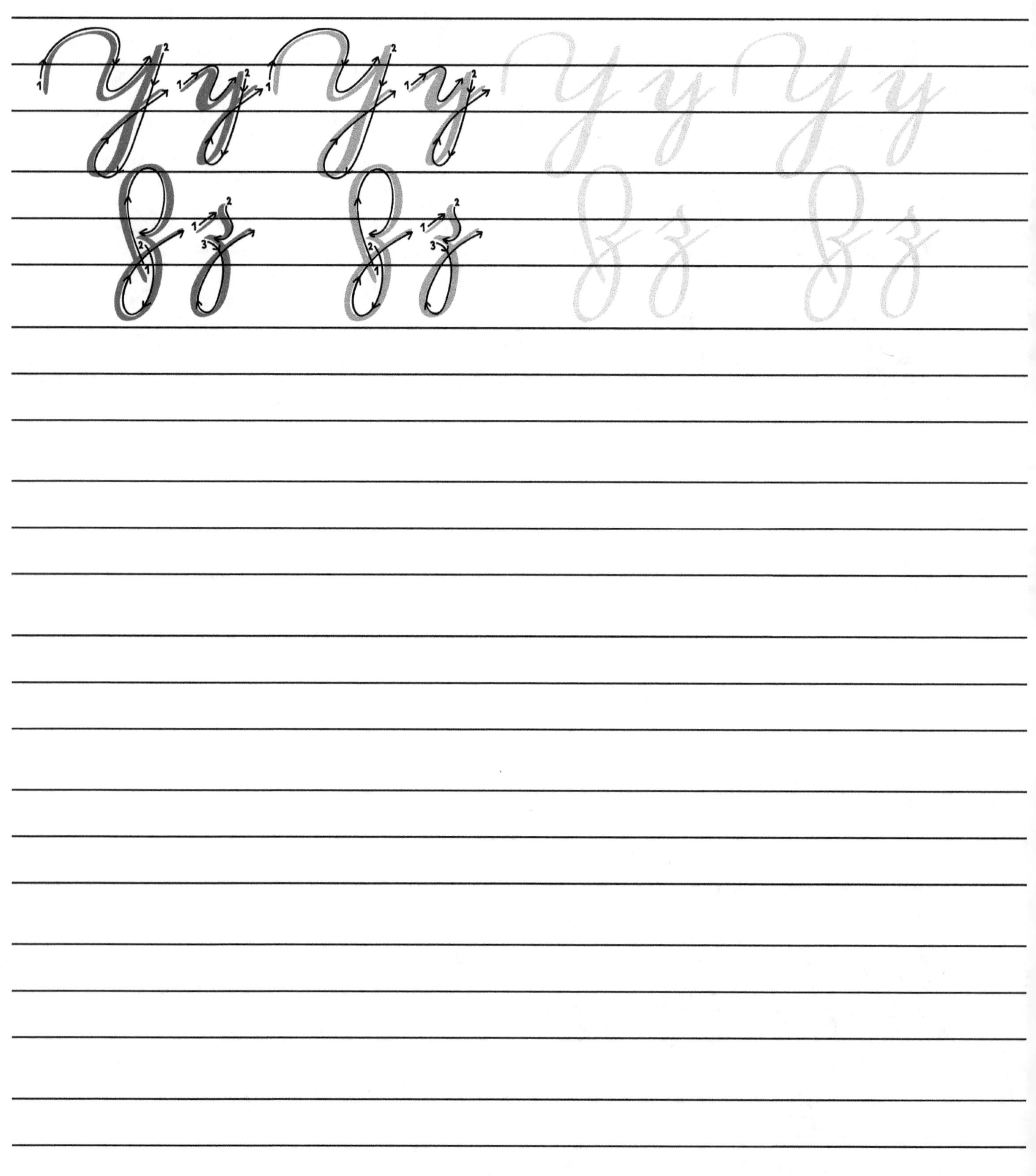

00000 111111

22222 333333

44444 555555

66666 777777

88888 99999

January January
January January
February February
February February
March March
March March
April April
April April

May May May

June June June

July July July

August August

September September

September September

October October

October October

November November

November November

December December

December December

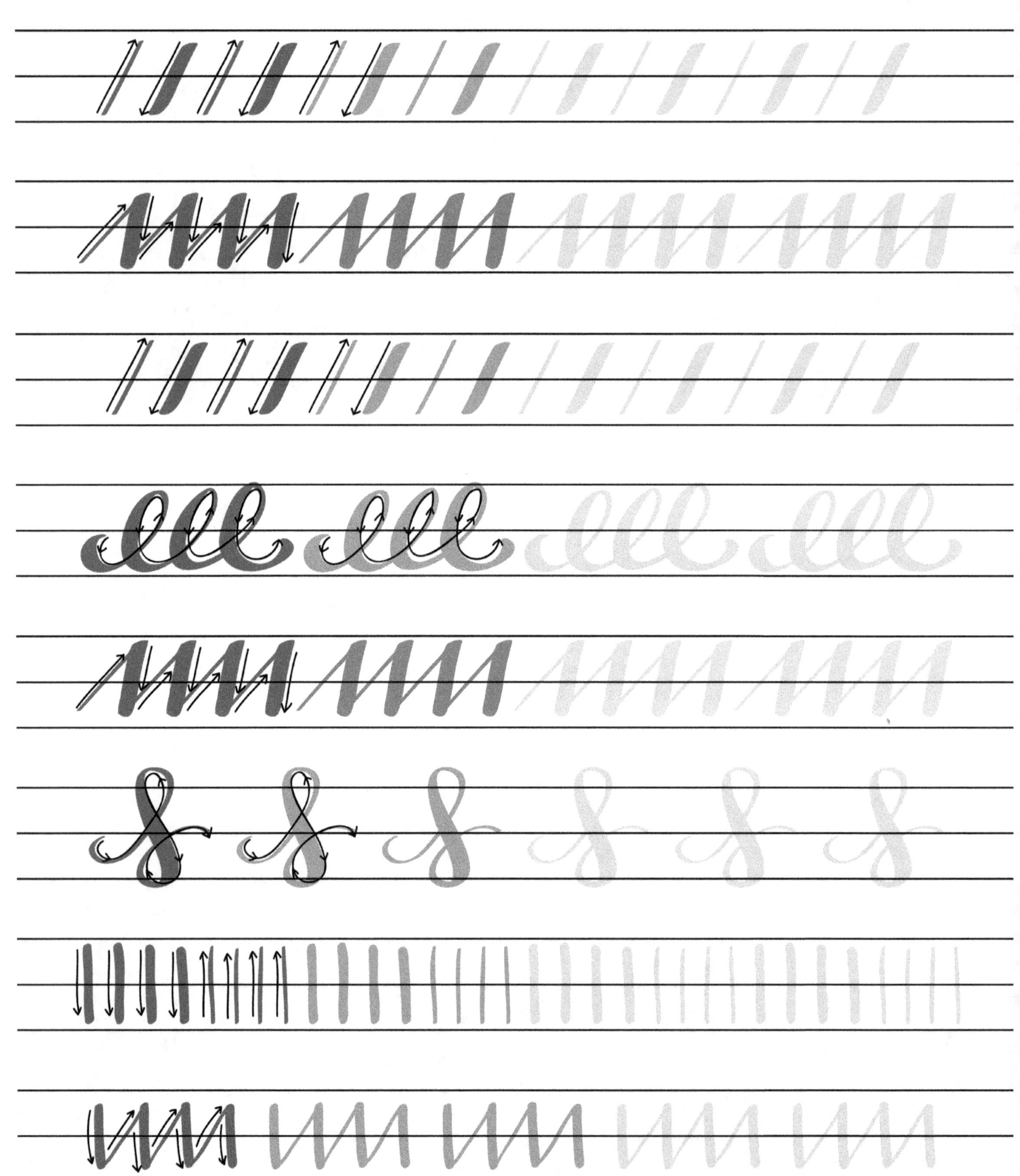

Genitals

Genitals

Genitals

Horny Horny

Horny Horny

Hard-on

Hard-on

Hard-on

Inches Inches

Funk Funk

Riss Riss Riss

Rinky Rinky

Rinky Rinky

Lap dance

Lap dance

Lap dance

Lick Lick Lick

Lick Lick Lick

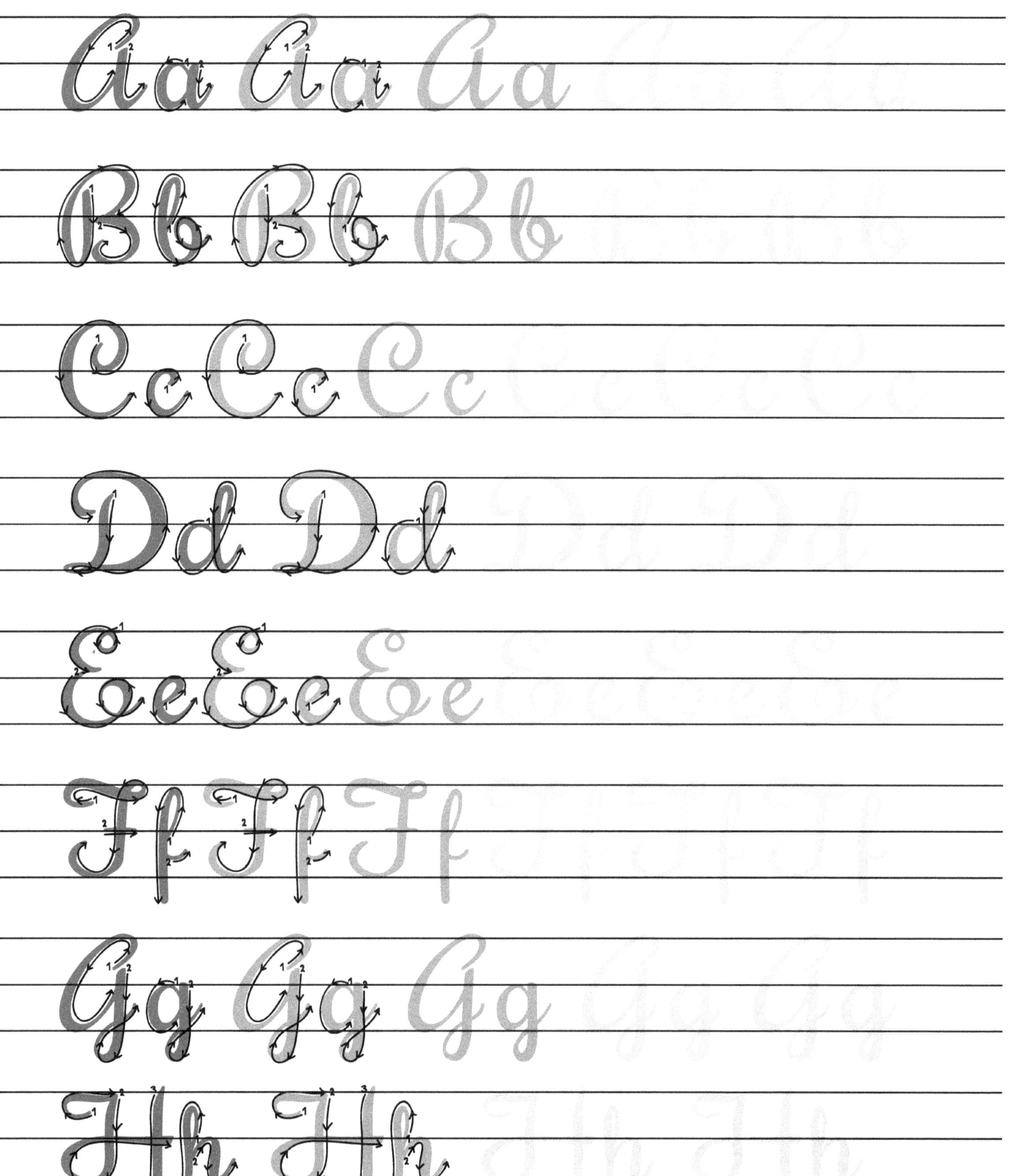

Ii Ii Ii Ii Ii Ii Ii

Jj Jj Jj Jj Jj Jj Jj

Kk Kk Kk Kk

Ll Ll Ll Ll Ll Ll

Mm Mm Mm Mm

Nn Nn Nn Nn Nn

Oo Oo Oo Oo Oo

Pp Pp Pp Pp Pp

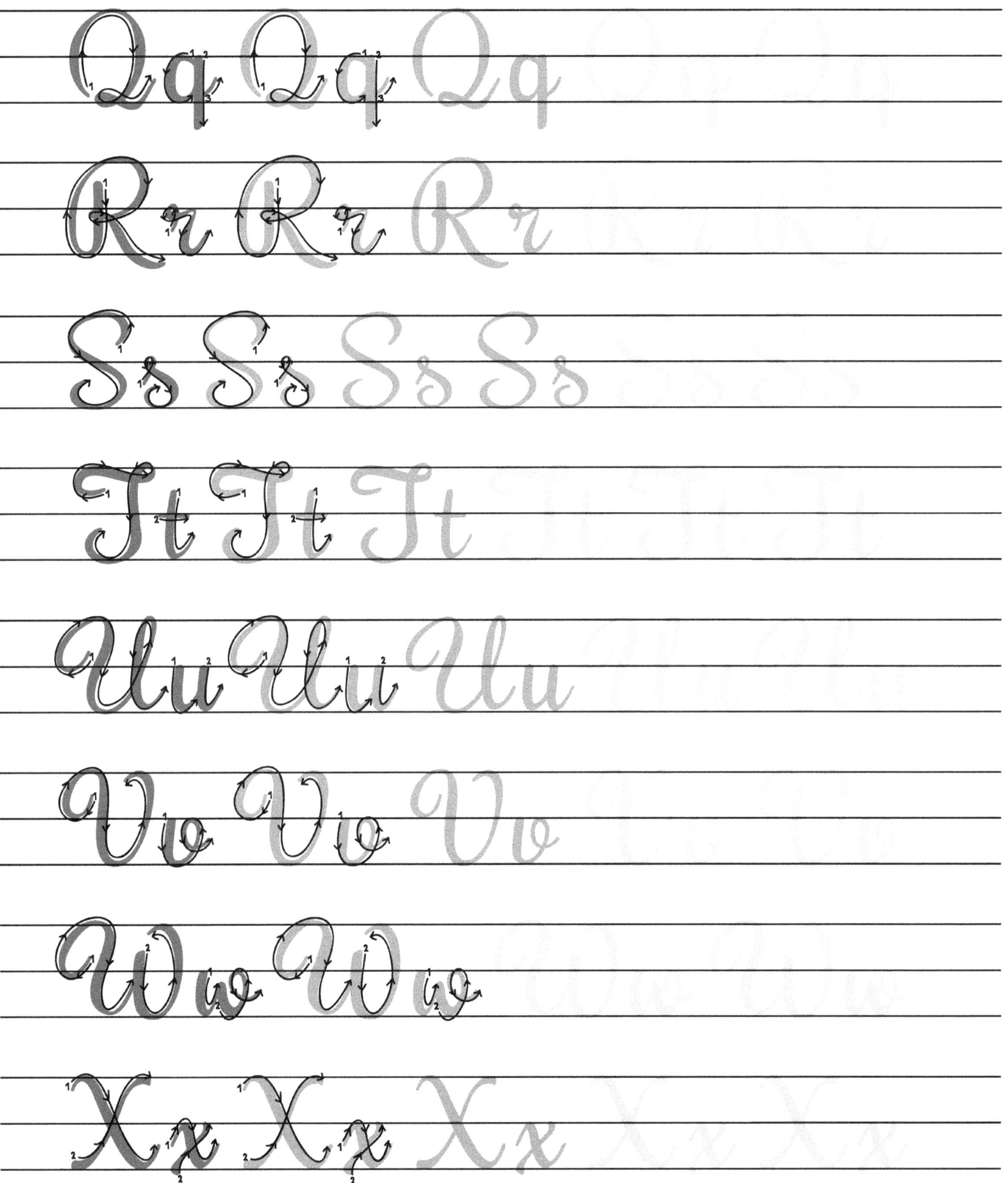

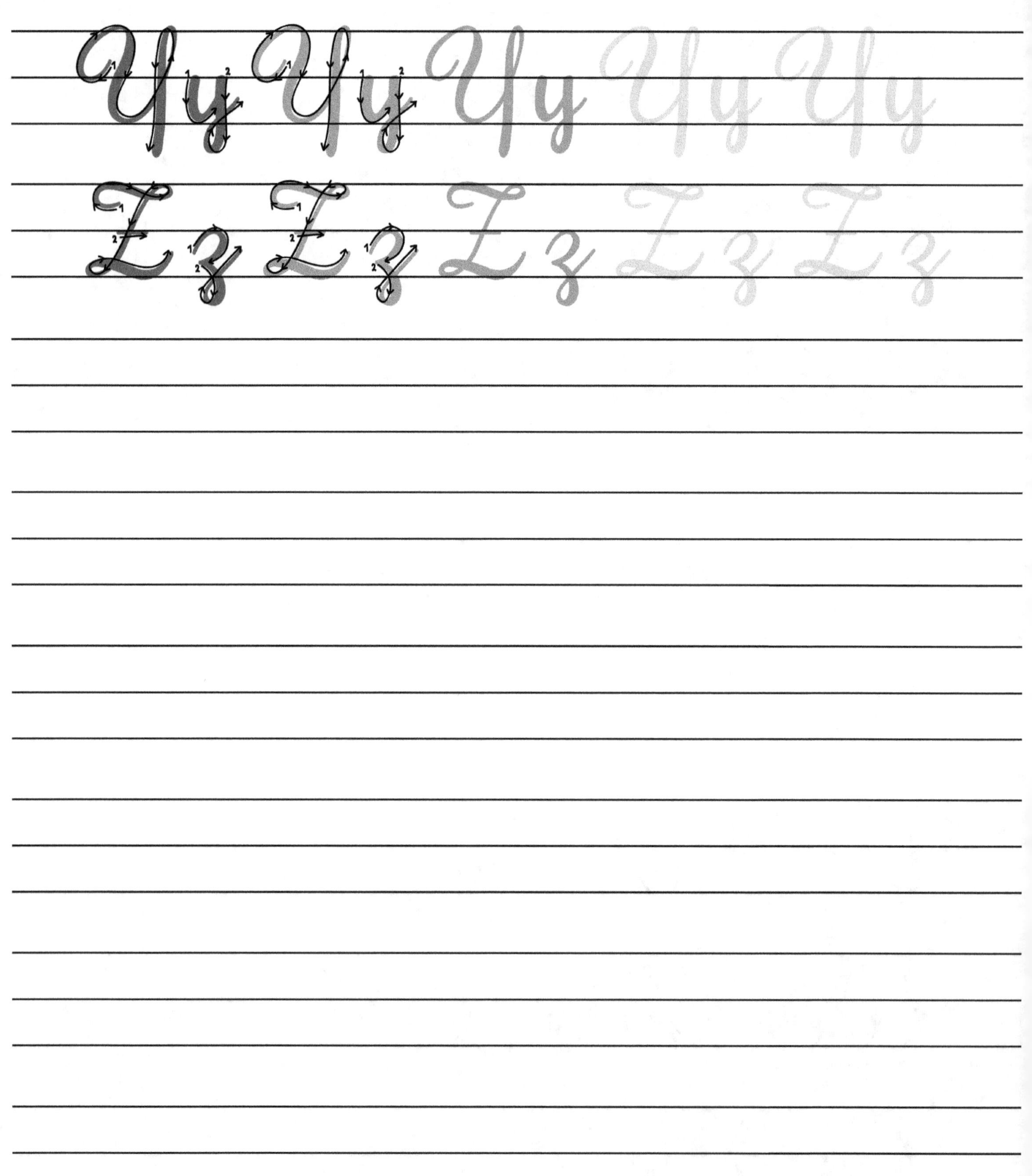

000000 111111

222222 333333

444444 555555

666666 777777

888888 999999

January January
January January
February February
February February
March March March
March March March
April April April
April April April

May May May

May May May

June June June June

June June June June

July July July July

July July July July

August August August

August August August

September September

September September

October October

October October

November November

November November

December December

December December

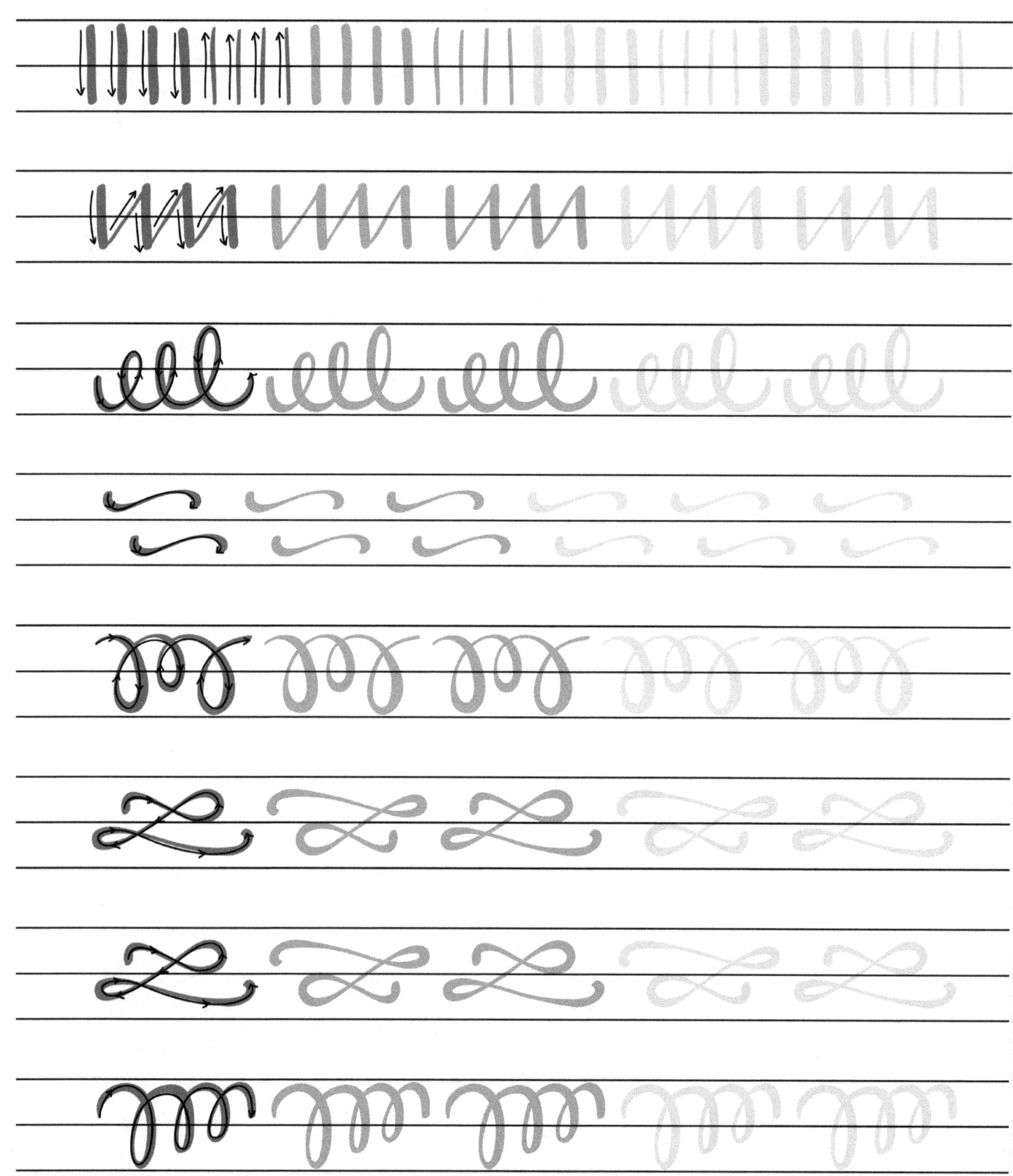

Lingerie Lingerie

Lingerie Lingerie

Lube Lube Lube

Lube Lube Lube

Magnum Magnum

Magnum Magnum

Missionary

Missionary

Missionary

Moan Moan Moan

Moan Moan Moan

Masturbate

Masturbate

Masturbate

Nipple Nipple

Nipple Nipple

Orgasm Orgasm

Orgasm Orgasm

Oral Oral Oral

Oral Oral Oral

Aa Aa Aa Aa

Bb Bb Bb Bb

Cc Cc Cc Cc Cc Cc

Dd Dd Dd Dd

Ee Ee Ee Ee Ee Ee

Ff Ff Ff Ff Ff

Gg Gg Gg Gg Gg

Hh Hh Hh Hh

Ii Ii Ii Ii Ii Ii

Jj Jj Jj Jj Jj Jj

Kk Kk Kk Kk

Ll Ll Ll Ll Ll

Mm Mm Mm Mm

Nn Nn Nn Nn

Oo Oo Oo Oo Oo Oo

Pp Pp Pp Pp Pp

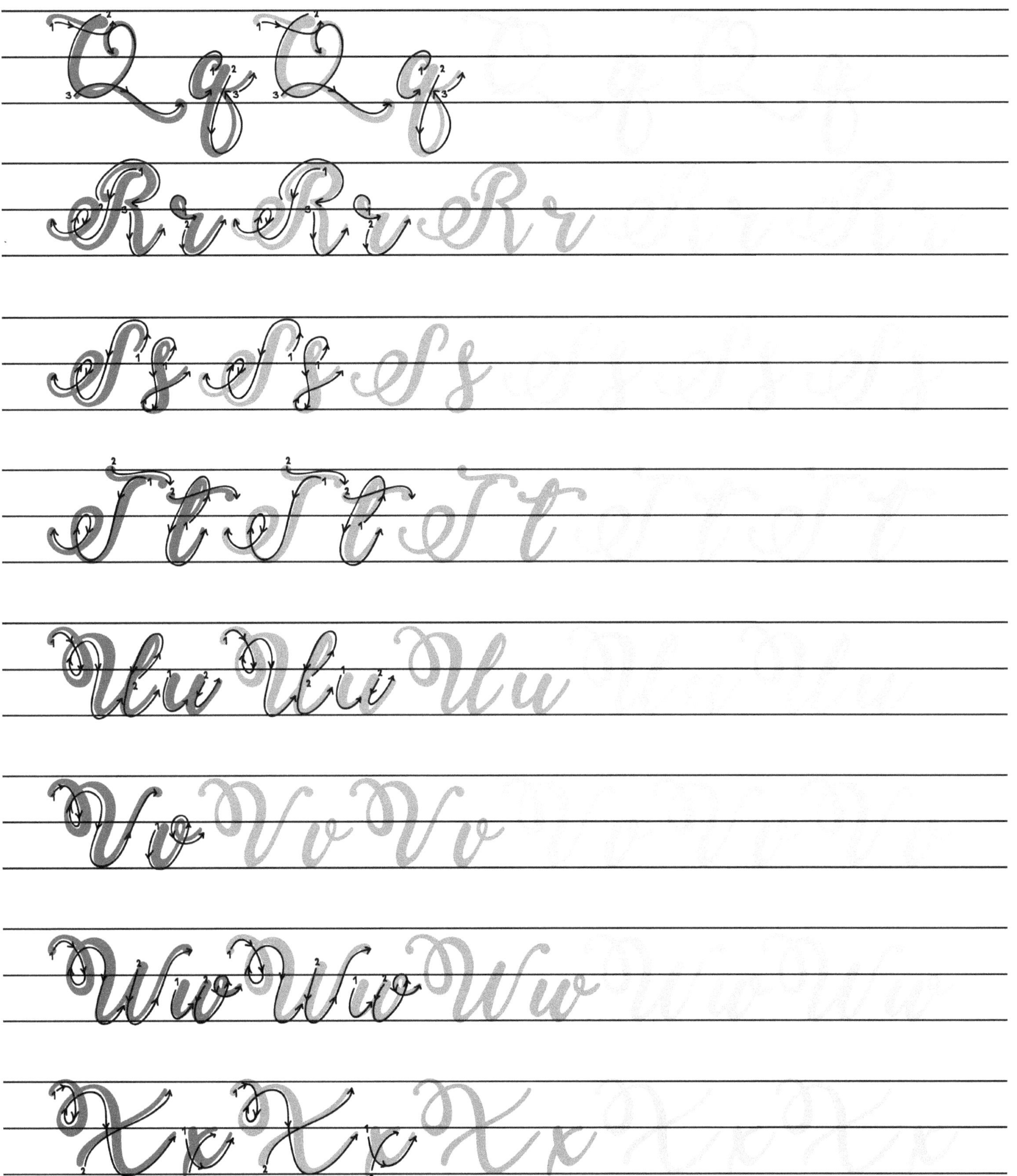

0000000 1111111

22222 333333

444444 555555

6666666 777777

8888888 999999

January January

January January

February February

February February

March March

March March

April April April

April April April

May May May
June June June
July July July
August August

September September

September September

October October

October October

November

November

November

November

December
December
December
December

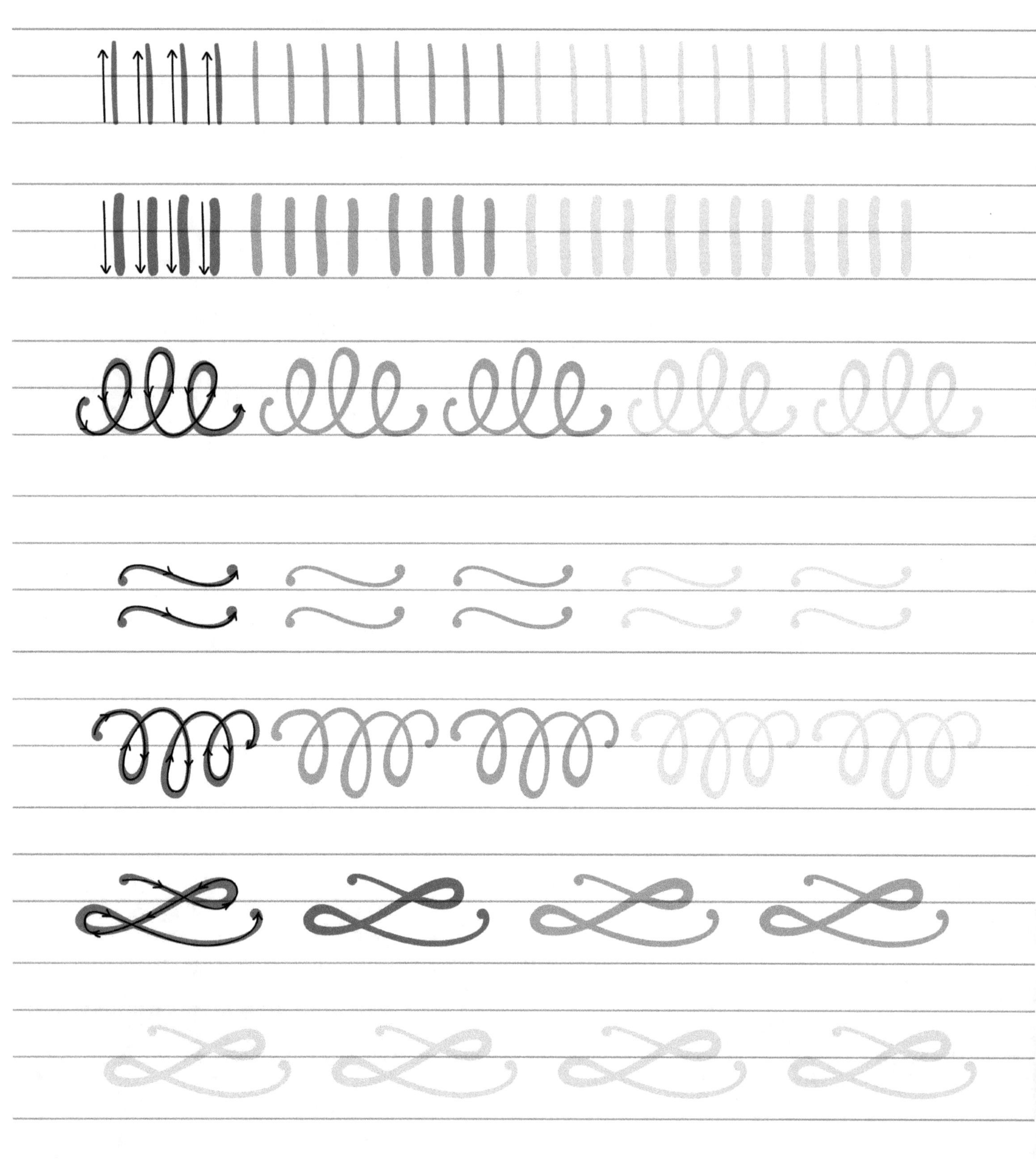

Pussy Pussy

Pussy Pussy

Penis Penis

Penis Penis

Penetrate

Penetrate

Penetrate

Queef Queef Queef

Rim Job

Rim Job

Sexy Sexy Sexy

Semen Semen

Semen Semen

Spank Spank

Spank Spank

Swinger Swinger

Swinger Swinger

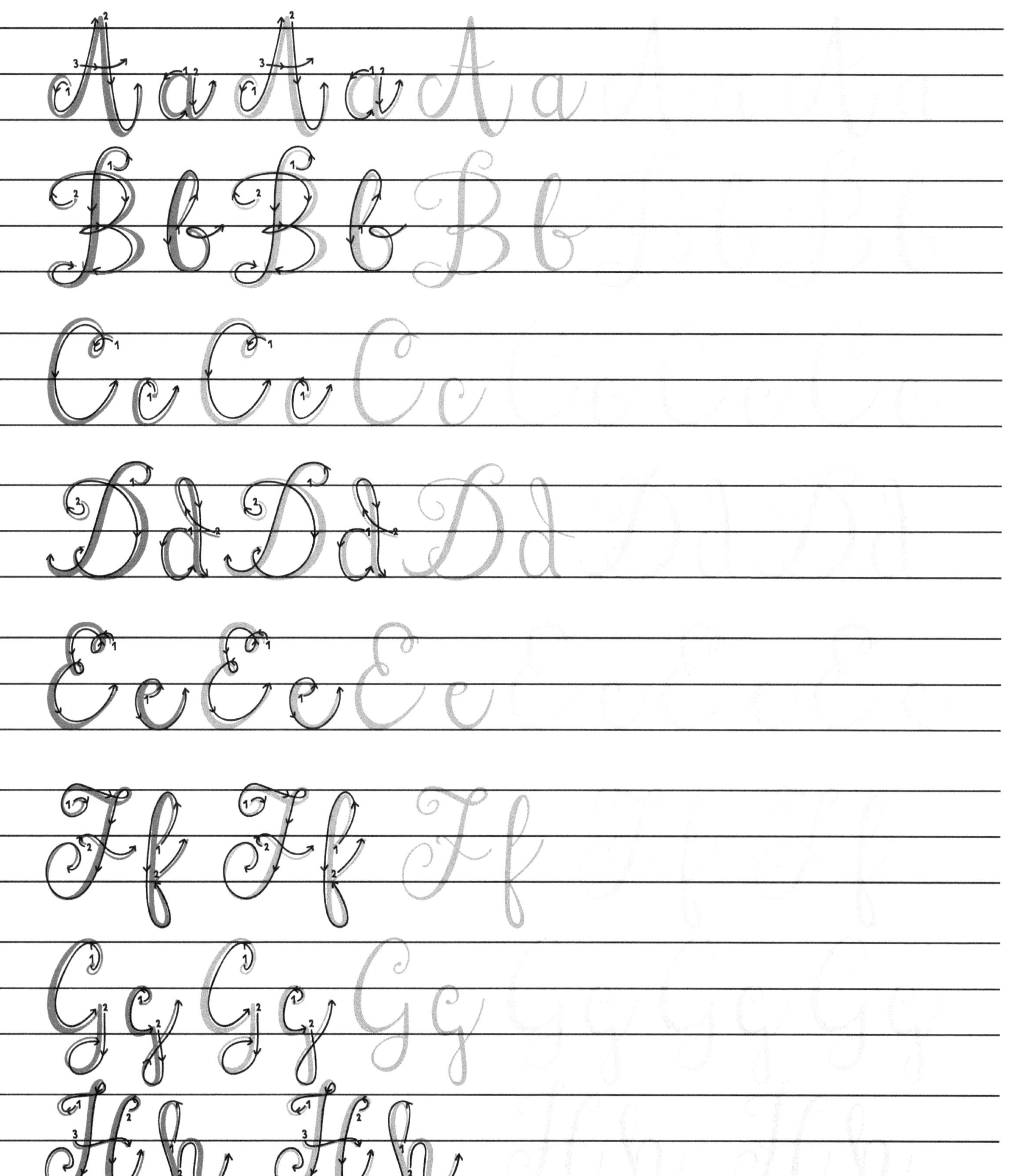

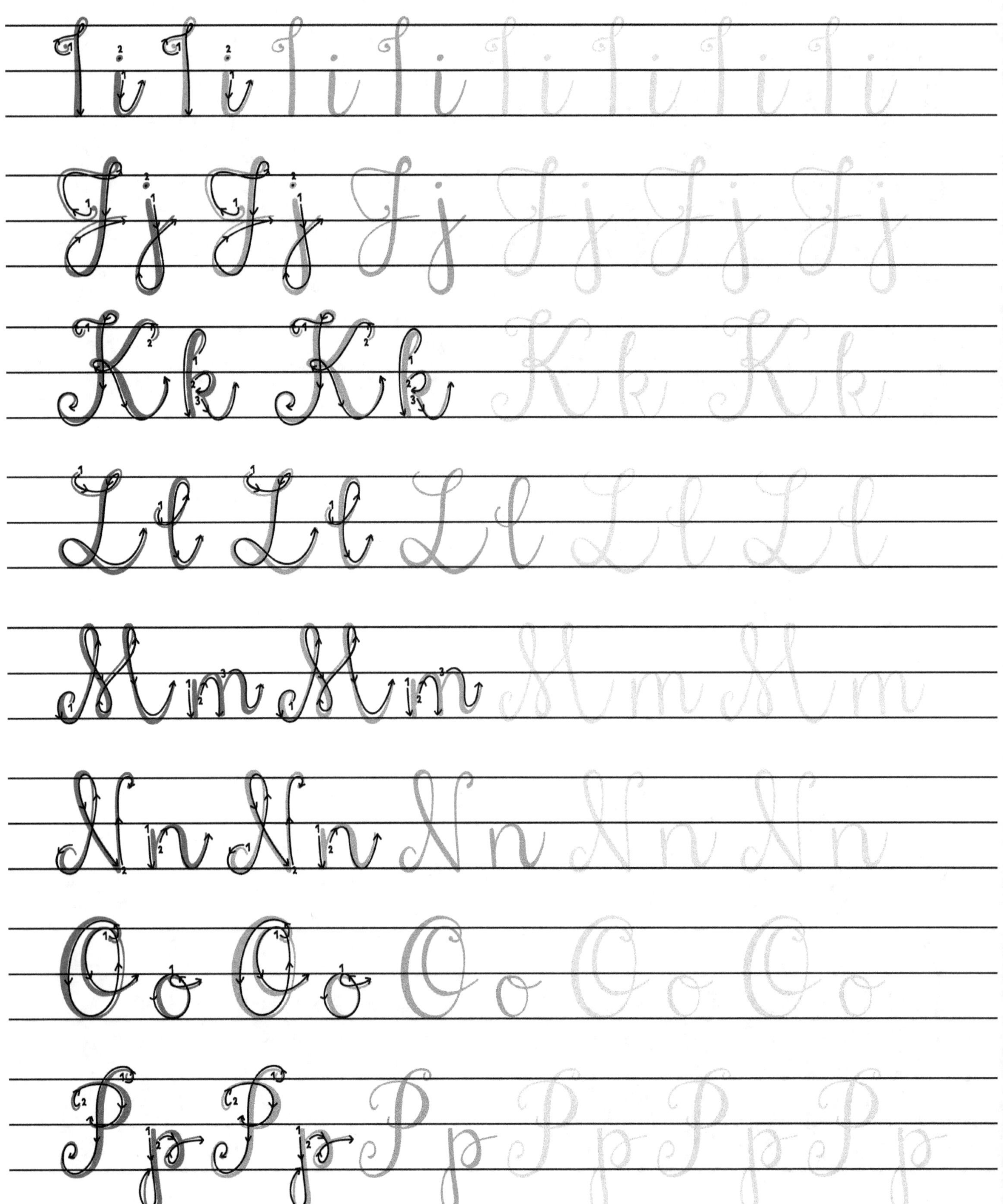

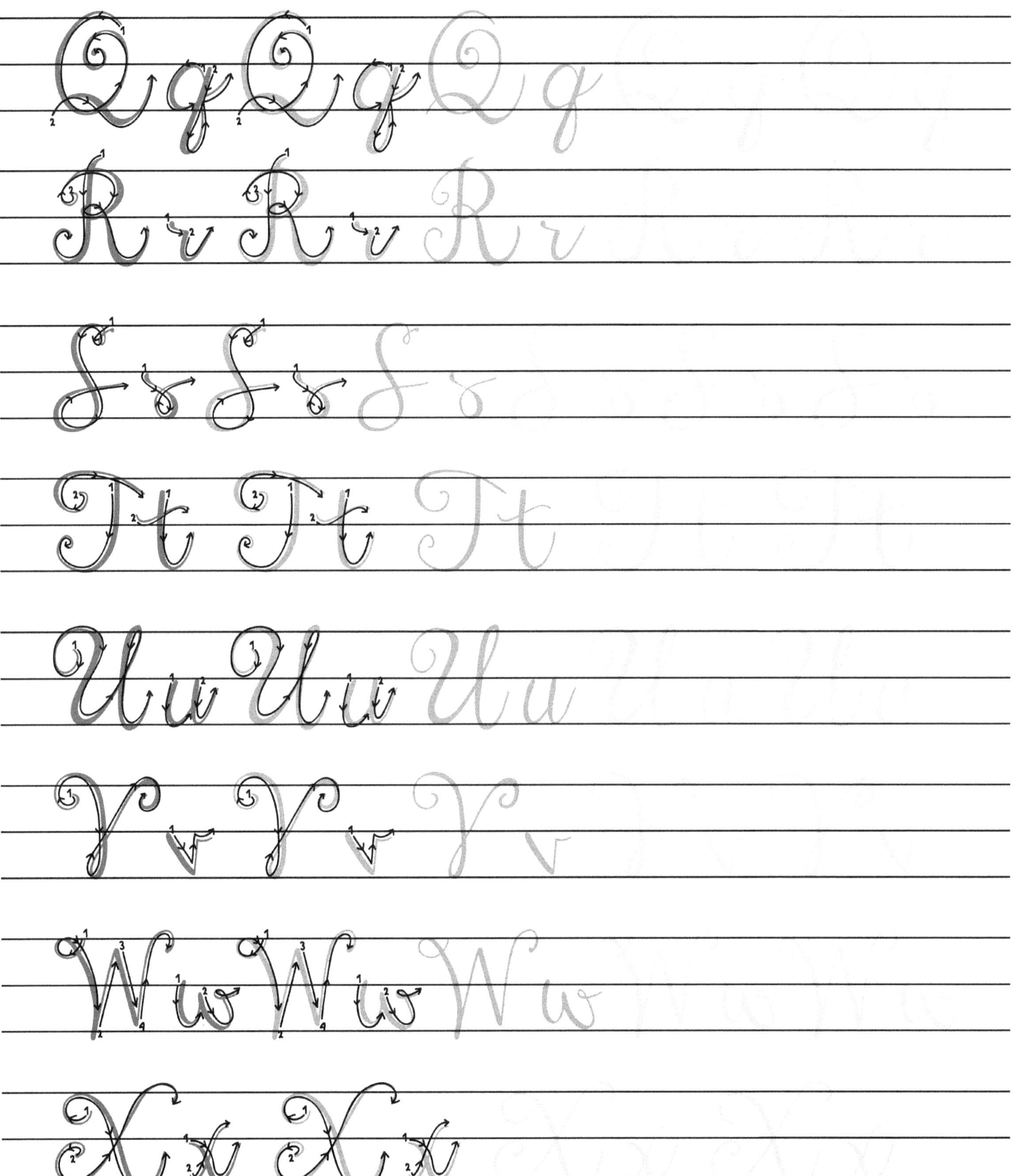

0000000 1111111

2222222 3333333

4444444 5555555

6666666 7777777

8888888 9999999

January January

January January

February February

February February

March March

March March

April April April

April April April

May May May

May May May

June June June

June June June

July July July

July July July

August August

August August

September September

September September

October October

October October

November November

November November

December December

December December

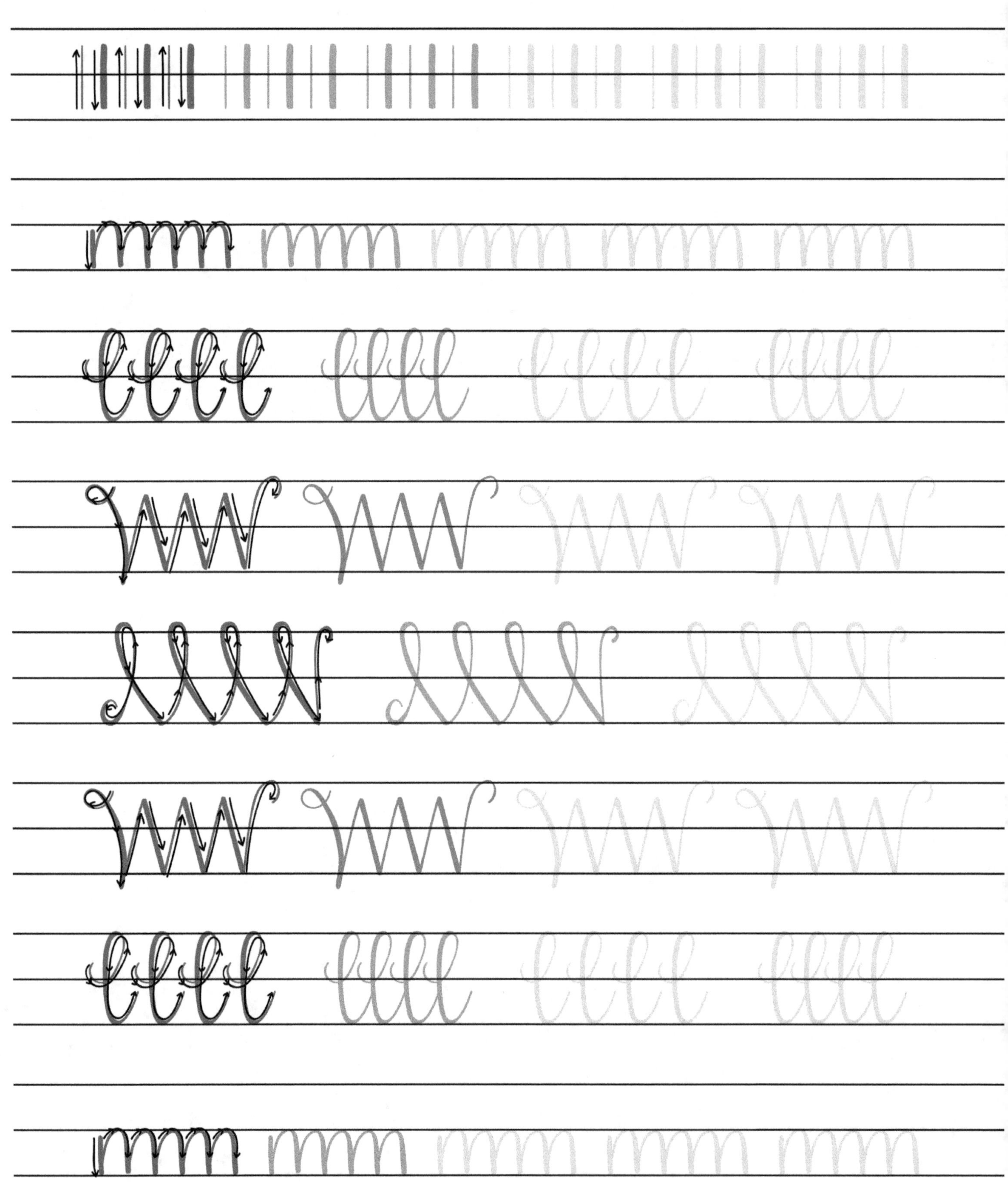

Tease Tease

Tease Tease

Threesome

Threesome

Threesome

Testicles Testicles

Testicles Testicles

Vaçina Vaçina

Vibrator Vibrator

Virçin Virçin

Wanking Wanking

Wanking Wanking

Wet Dreams

Wet Dreams

Wet Dreams

X-Rated X-Rated

X-Rated X-Rated

Check out our other books!

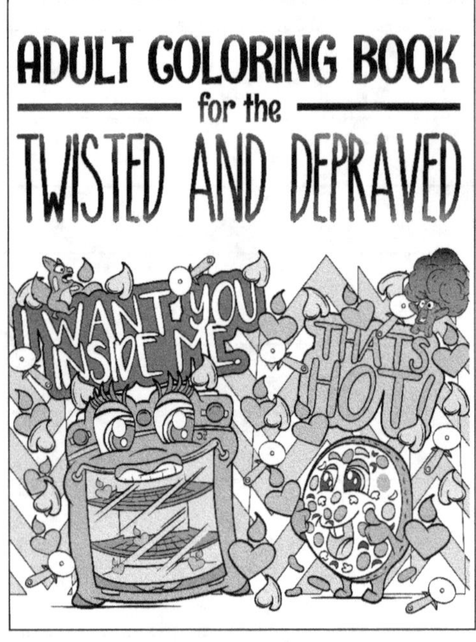

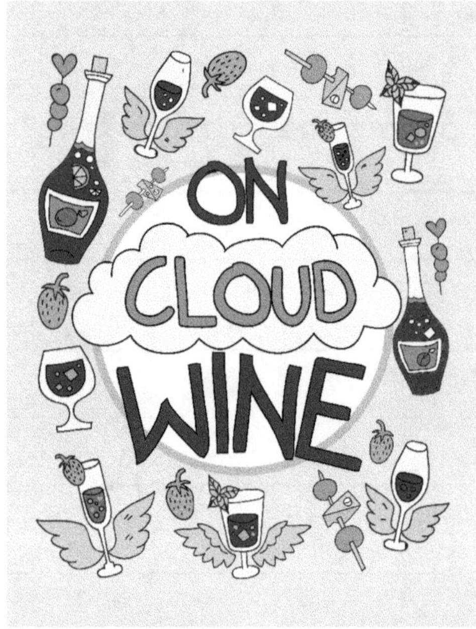

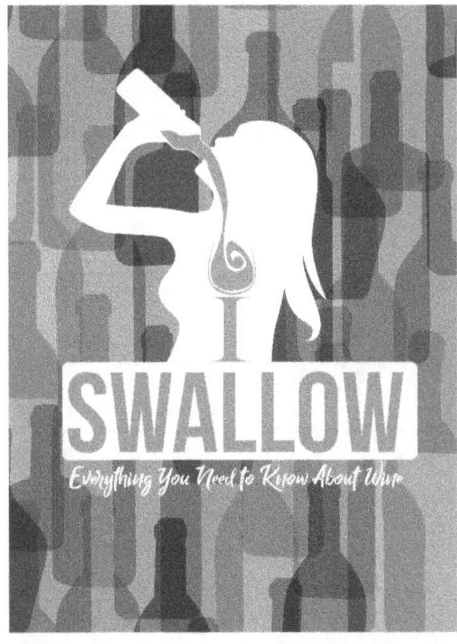

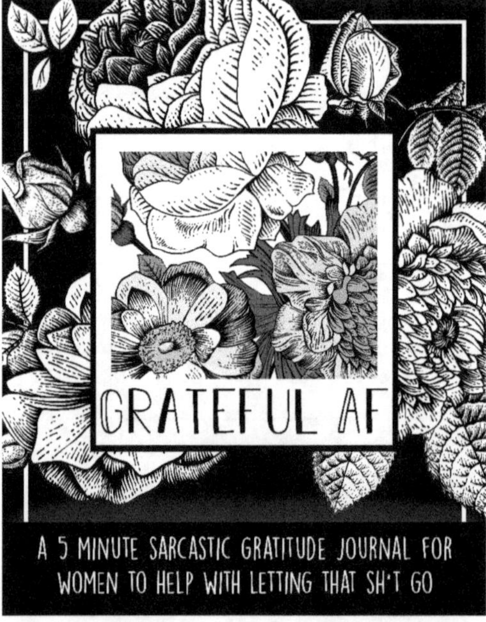

We would love for you to leave a review on Amazon!

www.ingramcontent.com/pod-product-compliance
Lightning Source LLC
LaVergne TN
LVHW081251100826
845148LV00009B/1197